GROSSET & DUNLAP
An imprint of Penguin Random House LLC
1745 Broadway, New York, New York 10019

First published in the United States of America by Grosset & Dunlap,
an imprint of Penguin Random House LLC, 2025

Text copyright © 2025 by WonderLab Group, LLC
Illustrations copyright © 2025 by Matthew Carlson

Photo credits: All photos courtesy of Shutterstock. Cover: (UP)
Maxal Tamor, (CTR) olpo, (LO) Sebastian Janicki; p. 3 (LE) Maxal
Tamor, (CTR) Sebastian Janicki, (RT) olpo; p. 5 (UP LE) photo-world,
(UP RT) Yes058 Montree Nanta, (LO LE) Maxal Tamor, (LO RT)
Sebastian Janicki; p. 7 (UP RT) OlegSam, (LO RT) TR_Studio; p. 8 (LO
LE) vvoe, (LO CTR) Yes058 Montree Nanta, (LO RT) Yes058 Montree
Nanta; p. 22 (UP LE) New Africa, (UP RT) Steve Cordory; p. 31 (UP)
mineral vision, (LO LE) vvoe, (LO RT) olpo

GROSSET & DUNLAP is a registered trademark of
Penguin Random House LLC.

Visit us online at penguinrandomhouse.com.

Library of Congress Cataloging-in-Publication Data is available.

Manufactured in China

ISBN 9780593890950   10 9 8 7 6 5 4 3 2 1 HH

The text is set in Santa Rosa, Museo Sans, and Canvas Text Sans.
The art in this book was created by a human. It was sketched on
paper, then drawn and painted in Adobe Fresco on an iPad.

Produced by WonderLab Group, LLC
Design by Rachael Hamm Plett, Moduza Design

TO GORIGNAK—PT

TO MAYA, MY ROCK, AND AVA AND
ANDERS, MY PEBBLES—MC

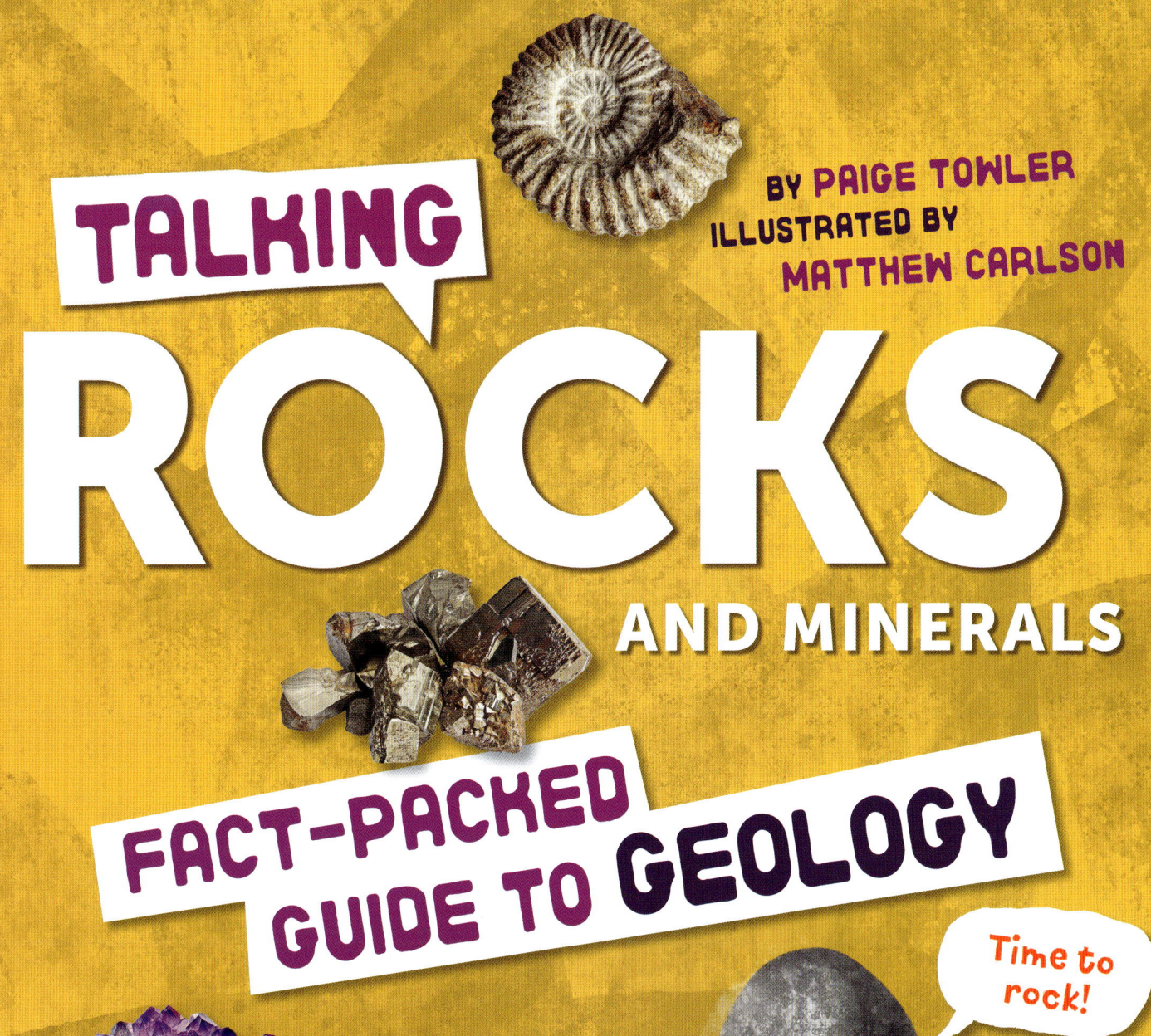

BY PAIGE TOWLER
ILLUSTRATED BY
MATTHEW CARLSON

TALKING
ROCKS
AND MINERALS

FACT-PACKED
GUIDE TO GEOLOGY

Time to rock!

GROSSET & DUNLAP

Hi, I'm Pebble.

I'm in constant conversation with the gems of geology. The rock stars rocking the rock world. The minerals making the mentions.

Do you know what makes rocks rock? Ace reporter Pebble is perfectly qualified to bring you the inside scoop.

Why? Like every rock, pebbles are made of **MINERALS,** or simple materials that make up the Earth. So, what are you waiting for? It's time to talk rocks—er, let those rocks talk.

IGNEOUS

EMERALD

PYRITE

GNEISS

SEDIMENT

VOLCANIC

GEODE

AMETHYST

FOSSILS

EROSION

ROCK FACE

There are three major types of rocks, grouped based on how they form. First up, **IGNEOUS ROCKS**.

Ready to ROCK, Granite?

I'm ready for my close-up, Pebble.

GRANITE'S STORY

I may look simple now, but long ago, I was hotter than hot—I was **MAGMA**.

Magma is superheated rock inside the Earth. When it reaches the Earth's surface, it becomes lava!

As magma, deep underground, I used to go with the flow.

But one day, I got stuck. Over millions of years, I cooled off. I hardened. I became me—Granite!

Other igneous rocks also form from cooling magma. Igneous rocks that form inside the Earth—like granite—are known as **INTRUSIVE**. Igneous rocks that form on the Earth's surface from lava are called **EXTRUSIVE**.

Wow, intense! Thank you—I'll never take you for GRANITE, buddy.

GRANITE is one of the strongest stones on Earth.

OBSIDIAN is an extrusive igneous rock that forms from lava. It has been used for thousands of years to make sharp tools.

COAL! LIMESTONE!
Do you have a minute to tell us the secrets of sedimentary rocks?

Why not? We were just lying around!

COAL

LIMESTONE

SEDIMENTARY ROCKS are some of the most common rocks on the planet. But there's more to them than that. In fact, millions of years ago, these rocks started out as tiny different pieces of material called sediment.

Coal forms from tiny pieces of plants that lived long, long ago.

calcite + dolomite = limestone

Limestone is made of two minerals.

COAL & LIMESTONE'S STORY

Sediment forms from tiny parts of many things, like plants, animals, minerals, and more.

Over time, this sediment collects and settles. It hardens, and more sediment collects on top. That hardens, too.

Eventually, the sediment forms sedimentary rocks—like us!

Pebble! What's rockin?

I'm on fire—that is, I'm reporting on igneous rocks. And sedimentary ones, too.

Hey, that's us!

GEODES can form in sedimentary or igneous rocks over thousands or even millions of years.

GEODES' STORY

Trickling water can hollow out spaces in sedimentary rocks to form us geodes.

We also form from gas bubbles trapped inside igenous rocks made from cooling magma.

AMETHYSTS take millions of years to form naturally as purple quartz. The oldest amethysts are older than the dinosaurs.

AMETHYST'S STORY

A volcano blew its top.

Lava flowed and bubbles of gas formed. The bubbles hardened into geodes.

Minerals collected in the geode's belly.

Gamma rays from the volcanic rock turned me purple!

BAM! I was born!

The largest known amethyst is called the Empress of Uruguay. It is more than 10 feet high and weighs over 5,000 pounds.

English and Russian royalty featured amethysts in crowns.

Let's roll on to discussing the last type of rock: **METAMORPHIC.**

I was going to chat with **MARBLE**, but Marble didn't want to be interviewed.

I changed my mind. I do that a lot, but I can't help it. I'm metamorphic! I brought a metamorphic friend, too. This is **GNEISS.**

Gneiss to meet you, Pebble.

METAMORPHIC ROCKS start out as sedimentary or igneous rocks. But over long periods of time and in certain conditions, they can change into metamorphic rocks.

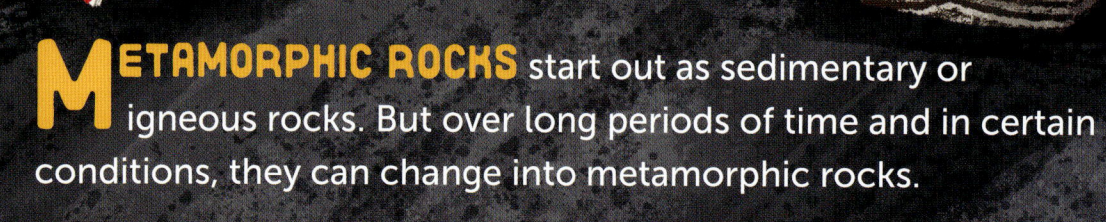

MARBLE'S STORY

I started out as limestone.

Then, it got really hot. I was under a lot of pressure.

WHAMMY!
I became marble.

GNEISS'S STORY

I can form from igneous or sedimentary rocks.

As long as I can withstand the heat and pressure, that is.

Good thing I thrive under pressure!

Does all this info make you feel like you're losing your marbles?

I'd never lose MARBLE!

Then get ready for the nitty-gritty on changing rocks.

Metamorphic rocks aren't the only rocks that undergo change. All rocks can be changed by water, heat, wind, and other factors.

Deep inside the Earth, extreme heat can melt all kinds of rocks down into magma.

Intense heat and pressure can turn all rocks into metamorphic rocks.

THE ROCK

That sediment can create new sedimentary rocks.

CYCLE

Then, when that magma cools, it might become a new igneous rock!

Come back sometime, we'll rock out!

These changes are known as the ROCK CYCLE— that's a great name for a band!

Wind and water can break down, or erode, any mountains, boulders, rocks, and stones into sediment.

17

Now let's go speak with some unusual rocks that can be hard to find.

Speaking of which... **DIAMOND?** Where are you?

Tee-hee. Here I am!

GEMS, like diamonds, are minerals or rocks that have been cut and polished to become shiny. They are valuable because they are not as common as regular rocks.

DIAMOND'S STORY

I formed from a mineral made of a substance called carbon.

Deep, deep in the Earth, pressure and heat squeezed me until...

I became a diamond in the rough. Before we're polished, gems look like any other rock.

Thousands of years ago, some people thought diamonds formed when lightning struck the earth.

Diamonds come in 12 colors, including pink, blue, and green.

But then, ta-da! I cleaned up nicely as a dazzling diamond!

Thanks for telling me all about diamonds. Shine on!

Gems come in many different varieties. Some gems form when minerals experience high heat and pressure. Others form when water seeps into rocks, carrying minerals with it.

WOW, it got bright out—no wait, those are more gems!

20

THE GEMS' STORY

EMERALDS are made of a mineral called beryl.

beryl

+

chromium

vanadium

=

Me!

SAPPHIRES are made of a mineral called corundum. When other materials are also present, we can become many different colors!

I'm green with envy! Are you feeling blue, Sapphire?

Not always!

For example, when a sapphire contains chromium, it makes something different...

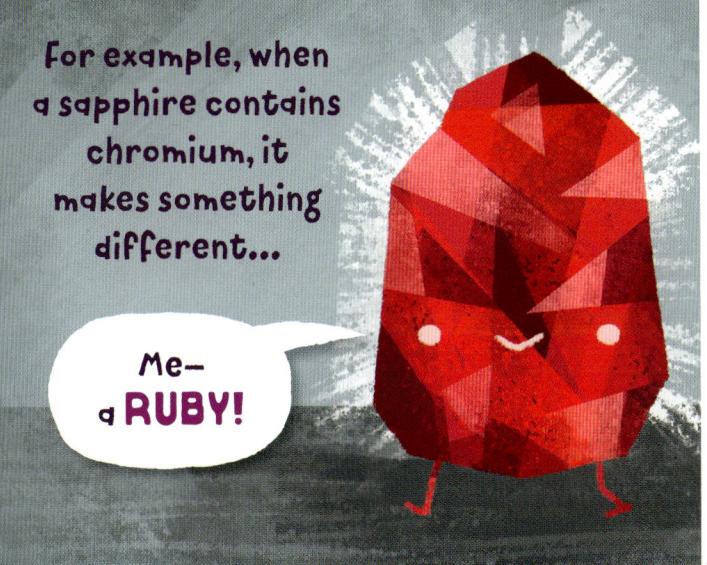

Me— a **RUBY!**

Priceless! But gems aren't the only valuable minerals found in nature...

Gold is a soft metal that is valuable to many people because it is used as money.

PYRITE is a type of mineral known for its shiny golden color. In the 1840s, people discovered gold in California.

PYRITE'S STORY

pyrite

gold

People rushed to California to get some gold for themselves. Instead, many people found me—Pyrite! But because I wasn't worth a lot like gold, they gave me the name "fool's gold."

When pyrite is struck with metal or stone, it can give off a spark. It can be used to help start fires.

As it turns out, there is gold inside of me—it's just in tiny amounts.

Maybe all that glitters really IS gold!

Fossils are the preserved remains and traces of living things that died long ago.

FOSSIL'S STORY

A long time ago, a dinosaur died and was quickly covered in sediment.

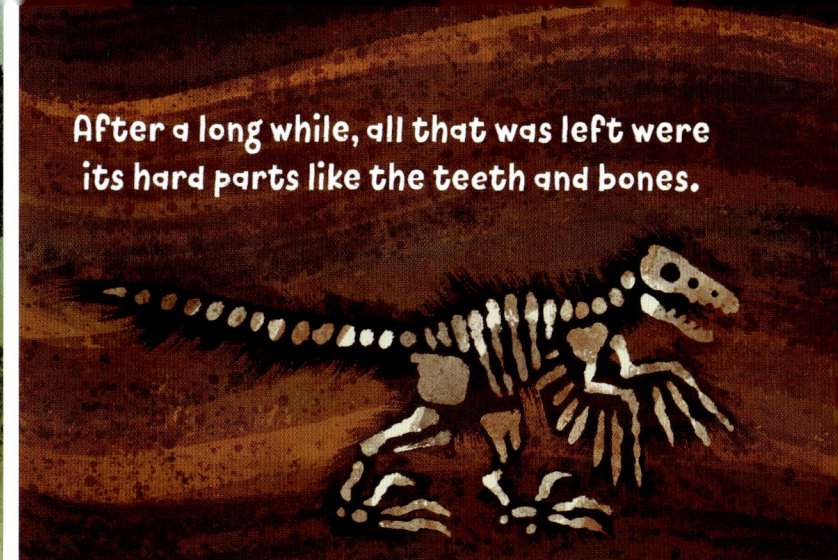

After a long while, all that was left were its hard parts like the teeth and bones.

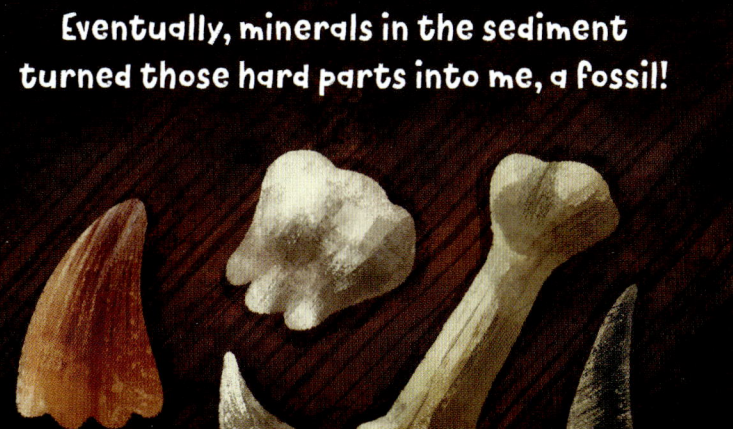

Eventually, minerals in the sediment turned those hard parts into me, a fossil!

We fossils can happen in other ways, too. When a soft plant decays, minerals can harden into rock around it and preserve its shape.

Or a footprint left in soft sand or mud can fill with sediment that hardens into rock—in the shape of the footprint.

Hardcore. Rock on, Fossil.

25

ASTEROIDS are rocks in space and METEORITES are space rocks on Earth.

METEORITES' STORY

We were asteroids, rocks traveling through space and around the Sun.

Pieces of us broke off and headed to Earth. Many asteroids burn up in Earth's atmosphere.

But we made it through and reached the ground.

You meteorites are really out of this world!

Some meteorites contain diamonds and other gems.

Scientists have found meteorites on Earth that may have come from other galaxies.

Most meteorites are billions of years old.

BACK IN MY DAY...

From rock stars rocking the rock world to rocks from the stars rocking the Earth world, you've nearly seen it all. Of course, there are always more rocks to discover!

This is Pebble, signing off for now— keep rocking on!

29

GLOSSARY

AMETHYST A crystal formed from purple quartz

ASTEROID A rocky object that travels through space

COAL A sedimentary rock formed from tiny pieces of ancient plants

CRYSTAL A solid formation with a geometric shape and flat surfaces, often made of minerals

DIAMOND A gem made from carbon

EMERALD A gem formed from beryl, chromium, vanadium, and sometimes iron

EXTRUSIVE ROCK An igneous rock that forms on the Earth's surface

FOSSIL The preserved remains or traces of a living thing that died long ago

GEM A mineral or rock that has been cut and polished to become valuable

GEODE Igneous or sedimentary rocks that contain crystalized minerals

GNEISS A metamorphic rock formed from many types of igneous or sedimentary rocks

GOLD A soft, valuable metal and mineral

GRANITE An igneous rock made mostly of quartz and feldspar

IGNEOUS ROCK A rock formed from magma or lava

INTRUSIVE ROCK An igneous rock that forms inside the Earth

LIMESTONE A sedimentary rock formed from calcite and dolomite

MAGMA Superheated rock inside the Earth

MARBLE A metamorphic rock formed from limestone

METAMORPHIC ROCK A rock transformed by intense heat and pressure

METEORITE A space rock that reaches Earth's surface

MINERAL A simple substance that makes up the Earth

OBSIDIAN An extrusive igneous rock that forms from lava

PYRITE A gold-colored mineral, also called "fool's gold"

ROCK CYCLE The changes that form and break down all rocks

RUBY A gem formed from corundum and chromium

SAPPHIRE A gem formed from corundum

SEDIMENT Tiny pieces of materials including plants, animals, minerals, and more

SEDIMENTARY ROCK Rocks formed from hardened sediment

FIND OUT MORE

For more information on rocks and minerals, check out these books:

Ultimate Rockopedia: The Most Complete Rocks & Minerals Reference Ever, Steve Tomecek

An Anthology of Rocks and Minerals: A Collection of Rocks, Minerals, and Gemstones from Around the World, DK

The Rock and Gem Book: And Other Treasures of the Natural World, DK and Smithsonian Institution

Rocks and Minerals Ultimate Handbook: The Need-to-Know Facts and Stats on More Than 200 Rocks and Minerals, Devin Dennie

The Fact-Packed Activity Book: Rocks and Minerals: With More Than 50 Activities, Puzzles, and More!, DK

Everything Rocks and Minerals, Steve Tomecek

Absolute Expert: Rocks & Minerals, Ruth Strother

Quiz Yourself Clever! Rocks and Minerals, DK

NOTE FROM A GEOLOGIST

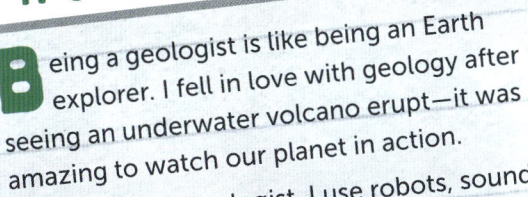

Being a geologist is like being an Earth explorer. I fell in love with geology after seeing an underwater volcano erupt—it was amazing to watch our planet in action.

As a marine geologist, I use robots, sound waves, and special tools to discover hidden treasures beneath the ocean. We even find gases that smell like rotten eggs!

Geologists have the coolest job because we explore places no one has ever seen and learn incredible things about our world. Every day is a new adventure, and that's why I love being a geologist.

—**ALDEN DENNY,**
marine geologist

BE A ROCK HOUND!

Check out these tips and tricks to get started on your journey as a rocking rock expert:

KEEP A ROCK JOURNAL Keep notes on the awesome rocks you find. Make sure to add sketches and detailed descriptions.

START A PHOTOGRAPHIC COLLECTION Take photos of cool or unusual rocks you find. Make sure to record the date and write a description of where you found the rock.

JOIN A CLUB See if there are local rock-lovers' clubs in your area. If there are none, consider starting one!

GET THE SCOOP ON GEOLOGY Read books about geology, and see if you can learn more about the local geology in your area.

TAKE A TUMBLE Some rock tumbling kits let you polish rocks yourself!

MEET THE CREATORS

AUTHOR

PAIGE TOWLER is a children's book author and poet living in Washington, DC. She loves writing scary stories, tales about animals, and nonfiction facts about the weird and wonderful world around us. Her previous picture books include *Mysterious, Marvelous Octopus* (National Geographic Kids), *Baby Bat Bedtime* (Smithsonian Institution/Sleeping Bear Press), *Yoga Animals* (National Geographic Kids), and more.

ILLUSTRATOR

MATTHEW CARLSON is an illustrator, game designer, and graphic designer in Northern California. He studied art and English literature at the University of California, Berkeley. He's illustrated projects for Robert Mondavi Wines, Facebook, and Twitter (now X), and is currently the Director of UX Design for Education, Fonts, and Drawing & Painting at Adobe. Matthew has never met a rock he didn't like, and spends his free time combing the local beaches and trails for interesting specimens. Originally from Seattle, Washington, Matthew now lives in Marin, California, with his partner, two kids, two dogs, and a growing collection of rocks.